# MINUTE MEDITATIONS

## FOR EVERYDAY CALM

Tamara Skyhawk

# PRAISE FOR

*Minute Meditations for Everyday Calm*

"These meditations will help you feel a deep sense of calm, no matter what is happening outside of you. They're quick, effective and so needed in a world that feels a bit busy, distracting, and often disconnected."

**– Sandy Alemian, Spirit Medium; Spiritual Guide, sandyalemian.com**

"A perfect match for the "too-busyness" of our lives—these meditations are short, simple, effective, and enjoyable. As someone who's in the business of helping other people slow down, I'm always on the lookout for easily sharable guidance for managing pain, overwhelm, and energetic fatigue. This book is an indispensable resource for teachers—a welcome addition to classrooms, yoga studios, retreats, and corporate wellness routines—but it's also accessible to self-help journeys and personal practices. Every meditation is a yummy morsel that enriches and enlivens awareness."

**– Alicia Delaney, RYT 200, Slow & Steady Yoga**

"Tamara does it again! Minute Meditations for Everyday Calm is my go-to guide for not only myself, but for working with clients. As someone who has a very full life, this book is a valuable way to commit to having meditation as part of my daily routine to keep my nervous system regulated. I appreciated how the sections were broken down and made it convenient to access meditations for body, mind, energy or emotions & feelings based on what is needed in that moment. These meditations are a great way to ground your client before, during or at the end of a session, no matter what profession you are in. They are easy to understand and easy to guide. Great resource for both beginners and experts. Highly recommend it!"

– **Amanda Welton, Owner & Holistic Anxiety Coach, Lavender Tusk**

"This book is for EVERYBODY!!! Anybody who needs to release stress and relax"

– **Yuko Kubokawa, Yoga Teacher and Student**

# Minute Meditations

## FOR EVERYDAY CALM

55 QUICK MEDITATION AND
MINDFULNESS PRACTICES FOR INSTANT
RELAXATION AND REFRESHMENT

Tamara Skyhawk

# CONTENTS

# AUTHOR'S NOTE

As someone who's practiced and taught meditation for over 20 years, I've witnessed the growing interest in meditation to manage stress, emotions and physical discomfort.

I've also seen that there are barriers to taking advantage of the benefits of those practices. Some people are new to meditation and don't know where to start, while others, myself included, have experience with meditation, love it, but don't always have the time or presence of mind for long meditation sessions. I created this book to solve both these issues. It's a book full of quick little meditations of just one to a few minutes long, that you can use anytime throughout your day to relax, reset and refresh. And, I've made it *very* simple.

Many meditation books present a series of steps you have to read, internalize and then practice. I wanted to simplify things even further, by leading you into states of relaxation and revelation *as you read*, rather than expecting you to remember the instructions.

That's also good news if you're someone who leads, or wants to lead, guided meditations. These meditations, mindfulness practices and relaxation techniques can be used as guided meditation scripts, read aloud as-is – to your yoga students, clients, classroom or family.

I'd like you to know that I haven't simply written these meditations, I practice them. Over the years, I've had to manage chronic pain, anxiety, depression and panic disorder. You probably wouldn't guess it upon meeting me – and that's thanks to meditations like those in this book. I practice these and other short meditations, every day, multiple times a day. It allows me to keep a positive outlook, manage pain, manage anxiety and ultimately – live happier, with more peace.

That said, it's important to understand that these meditations are for life's everyday stresses, upsets, exhaustion, etc. They're not meant as a solution for serious depression, anxiety, panic or other significant mental health challenges. If you feel like you need help, I encourage you to reach out to a qualified mental health professional in your area. We all need a helping hand sometimes. And perhaps you'll find that these meditations are a helpful addition to a well-rounded treatment plan.

I sincerely hope these minute meditations help you live with greater happiness and peace, and that this book becomes a trusty companion for you at home, work or on the go.

Side Note: Some of these meditations include excerpts from my books, *Yoga Nidra Scripts* and *Yoga Nidra Scripts 2*. If you are looking for longer meditation scripts, you'll find them in those two books.

# TIPS FOR USING THIS BOOK

The nature of life is change, which means your meditation needs will naturally change, too. To give you a well-rounded experience, this book includes a diverse array of meditations, mindfulness practices and relaxation techniques to try in times of need.

I've arranged the meditations into four sections, to help you more quickly find the right meditation when you need it:

- For Your Body
- For Your Mind
- For Energy
- For Emotions & Feelings

Since we're all different, I expect some of the meditations will resonate with you and some will not. My hope is that after trying them all in the times that you need them, you'll discover the ones that really work for you – and because they're simple, you can easily remember them. Those will become your go-to collection of minute meditations to help you reset whenever you need. Like a toolbelt of teeny meditations always at the ready for you.

To help you keep a slow, reflective pace, I've used *(pause)* to indicate when you should pause for one slow breath, and *(long pause)* to indicate when to pause for three slow breaths.

In general, since these are meditations, they're meant to be read slowly. Also, feel free to close your eyes anytime you want to relish a peaceful sensation.

To hear samples of the pacing I use, visit **tamaraskyhawk.com/free** to get these three complementary meditations as mp3 audio recordings:

- Smile Lifter
- Candle Melt
- Slow Your Roll

Before you start reading a meditation, make a mental note that you're consciously taking a time out for a few minutes. This can help settle you. Consider keeping a clip with your book, to keep it open or upright so you can have a more relaxed, hands-free experience.  You can also add elements like essential oil to breathe in before you begin. The more you make these minute meditations a ritual, the easier it will be for you to ease into a state of peace and relaxation each time.

I hope these minute meditations will not only be enjoyable and easy for you, but a great help for bringing body, mind and soul back to balance quickly – whether you're using them for yourself or sharing them as a Yoga Teacher, Therapist, School Teacher, Parent or Caregiver.

# FOR YOUR BODY

# TENSION CHECK & RELEASE

*Become aware of which body parts are holding tension, so you can return to a state of ease.*

Sitting or lying comfortably, take a deep breath in and a long breath out.

Become aware of the forehead and eyes.

Notice if there is any tension there – any holding, squeezing, tightness?

Could you soften any part of the forehead or eyes?

Go ahead and soften any part of the eyes and forehead that you can. *(pause)*

Now become aware of the lips and jaw.

Notice if there is any tension there – any pursing, clenching, tightness?

Could you release, drop or soften tension in any part of the lips or jaw?

Go ahead and soften tension now, in the lips and jaw. *(pause)*

Become aware of the neck and shoulders.

Any tension?

Soften, drop, release. *(pause)*

Become aware of the hands.

Any tension in fingers, palms, wrists?

Soften and release. *(pause)*

Become aware of the hips.

Any gripping, tightness, tension?

Soften and release. *(pause)*

Become aware of the legs and feet.

Any squeezing, gripping, tightening?

Soften and release. *(pause)*

Now taking a moment to take stock.

Did you notice any areas of tension?

A lot, or even a little?

Simply be aware of it.

Make a mental note to check in with your body throughout the day, softening and releasing any areas where tension arises and disturbs your ease.

# SOLID, LIQUID, VAPOUR

*Transform heavy-feeling tension.*

---

If there's an area or part of your body that's tense, and the tension feels heavy or blocked, this is a great exercise to break it up.

First, allow awareness to rest on the area.

Tune in to the sensation of heaviness, denseness, solidity. *(pause)*

Maybe the area feels blocked… or is weighing you down.

Noticing the solidity, feel as if the area begins to liquify.

Solid to liquid.

Melting and liquifying.

Area becoming more fluid, lighter.

More subtle. *(pause)*

And now, becoming subtler still, tension vaporizes.

Liquid to vapour.

Up and out.

Away from your body.

Tension turned from solid, to liquid to vapour. *(long pause)*

Try on another area of the body now.

Noticing the tension.

Feel it as solid, heavy, dense. *(pause)*

And now, melt, liquify, loosen. *(pause)*

Finally, vaporize, diffuse, disperse. *(pause)*

Now light and free. *(long pause)*

Repeat this process with another area of tension if you like.

Solid… liquid… vapour. *(pause)*

Tension becomes more and more subtle, moving up and out. *(long pause)*

When all tension is vaporized, take a few moments of stillness to appreciate this new sensation of lightness, subtlety, freedom.

# LOVE & KISSES

*Show your body some love – with your sweet attention.*

Settling into any comfortable position.

Let your eyes become heavy.

Take a deep breath in.

And a long breath out.

Ready to begin the practice of moving awareness through the body, freely and effortlessly.

As you move awareness, you *automatically* give the sweet gift of your attention.

If you like, imagine you're giving a quick kiss or loving smile to each body part.

Your body receives this and feels comforted by it.

The simple, powerful gift of your attention, bringing comfort through the whole body.

Begin with awareness of the right hand.

Hello, right hand. Quick kiss or loving smile to the right hand.

Moving over to the left hand. Quick kiss or loving smile to the left hand.

And now shift awareness to the right wrist…. left wrist. Quick kiss or smile.

Right elbow… left elbow. Loving attention.

Right shoulder… left shoulder… back of the head near the top… crown of the head…the space between the eyebrows.

Right eye… left eye… right ear… left ear. Kisses or smiles.

Right cheek… left cheek… tip of the nose… upper lip… lower lip… chin.

Throat… heart… navel… right hip… left hip… right knee… left knee… right ankle… left ankle… right toes… left toes.

Awareness of the whole right side of the body.

The whole right side of the body, comforted by your attention. *(pause)*

Awareness of the whole left side of the body.

The whole left side of the body, comforted by your attention. *(pause)*

Awareness of the whole body together.

The whole body together.

The whole body together. *(pause)*

Held in the hug of your own loving attention, for as long as you like. *(long pause)*

# ROSE RELEASE FOR HEADACHES

*Release head tension in a beautiful way.*

Sitting or lying comfortably, inhale and exhale deeply.

Allow your awareness to arrive at a single point of tension on your head. Maybe the top of the head, base of the skull, forehead, eyes, temples, behind the ears… Choose any one point. The point that's calling you the most.

Or, if you feel your whole head crying out with tension, simply rest awareness on the top of your head.

Awareness on a single point on your head.

Allow the image of a tight rosebud to arise, emerging from that point. Tight rosebud – emerging from the centre of the tension.

Watch the rosebud rise slowly, then softly, begin to open.

As it does so, feel tension begin to release from that point.

Rosebud opening, blooming, more tension releasing.

Rose petals opening fully, all tension *released*. (pause)

Allow awareness to expand slightly, to the space around the bloom. Awareness of the space around the rose.

Visualize a crop of rosebuds rising up in the whole area.

Whole area blooming with roses, tension releasing. *(long pause)*

Now be aware of another area of tension on the head. *(pause)*

Holding awareness there, visualize a tight rosebud emerging.

Watch it slowly, softly begin to open, releasing tension. Releasing tension into the air, like releasing fragrance.

Rosebud opening, blooming, more tension releasing.

Rose petals opening fully, all tension *released*. *(pause)*

Expand awareness slightly, to the space around the bloom.

Awareness of the space around the rose.

Rosebuds are rising, blooming, releasing tension. *(long pause)*

Whole area in full bloom; tension released.

And now, visualizing all areas of your head blooming, releasing tension.

Top of the head, base of the skull, forehead, eyes, temples, behind the ears, sinuses, jaw… all points blooming, releasing.

Until your whole head is a beautiful crown of roses, free of tension.

Hold that sense of freedom for as long as you like.

If it feels liberating, go deeper into the sensation with eyes closed.

# TRIPLE-SCOOP SHOULDER TENSION RELEASE

*Three steps to deliciously release shoulder tension, anytime.*

Get comfortable, sitting up as straight as you can, on the floor or in a chair. *(pause for settling)*

If you feel you're slouching or could be sitting a little straighter, place a cushion, yoga block or folded blanket under your sitz bones, but not your thighs.

This can help release tension from your hips and back, allowing you to sit upright more easily.

1.

Once you're comfortable, roll your shoulders back slowly, in big circles.

Keep your chest lifted.

Use your full range of motion – all the way up, back, down and front.

Big circles, releasing tightness.

Breathe out any tension.

Do this three more times. *(long pause)*


2.

Now inhale, shrug your shoulders up to your ears.

Tense them up.

Hold 1… 2… 3.

Drop! Release all tension immediately.

Again, shrug your shoulders up.

Tense.

Hold 1… 2… 3.

Release!

One more time.

Tensing up the shoulders.

Hold 1… 2… 3.

Release.


3.

Finally, take three deep breaths. With each exhale, feel your shoulders becoming more relaxed and at ease, letting go of any effort. *(long pause)*

Enjoy the rest of your day!

# TRIPLE-SCOOP
# NECK TENSION RELEASE

*Three steps to deliciously release neck tension, anytime.*

Get comfortable, sitting straight. If you're slouching, place a cushion or block under your sitz bones, but not your thighs.

1.

Once you're comfortable, keeping your chin parallel to the floor, chest lifted, slowly look to the right.

Now slowly look to the left.

Slowly look right.

Slowly look left.

Slowly look right.

Slowly look left.

Bring your head back to centre.

2.

Now, keeping your chest lifted, slowly drop your right ear to your right shoulder.

Keep your shoulders relaxed.

Now slowly drop your left ear to your left shoulder.

Shoulders relaxed. Chest lifted.

Slowly back over to the right.

And over to the left.

One more time, right ear to the right shoulder.

And left ear to the left shoulder.

Bring your head back to centre.

3.

Finally, sitting tall, chest lifted, chin parallel to the floor, pull your chin straight back, without tilting it down or lifting it. You should feel some stretch in the back of your neck.

Hold 1… 2… 3.

Release.

Pull your chin straight back again.

Hold 1… 2… 3.

Release.

And last time, pull your chin straight back.

Hold 1… 2… 3.

Release.

Draw tiny spirals with the top of your head clockwise, then counterclockwise, loosening up. *(pause)*

Finish with three deep breaths, each exhale softening and releasing effort from your neck even more. *(long pause)*

# TRIPLE-SCOOP
# BACK TENSION RELEASE

*Three steps to deliciously release back tension, anytime.*

Get comfortable, sitting straight. If you're slouching, place a cushion or block under your sitz bones, but not your thighs.

1.

Rest your hands on your knees or thighs.

Hanging onto your thighs or knees, pull your elbows back, pressing your chest forward.

Now cave in your chest, rounding your back.

Inhale, lift your chest again. Hold.

Exhale, round your back. Hold.

Inhale, lift your chest one final time.

Hold 1… 2… 3.

And release.

2.

Now, keeping your hands on your knees or thighs, move your ribs, but not your shoulders, to the right and slightly up.

Now slide your ribs, but not your shoulders, over to the left and slightly up.

Ribs slide to the right. Hold.

Then left. Hold.

Right. Hold.

Then left. Hold.

And back to centre. *(pause)*


3.

Now, sitting tall, hands still on knees or thighs, lean your torso forward, tailbone lifted back.

Now lean, to the right.

Lean back, tailbone tucks under.

Lean left.

And back to the front, tailbone lifted.

Drawing slow circles with your torso, clockwise, three times.

Now reverse, circling counterclockwise three times.

And return to centre.

Finish with three deep breaths, each exhale softening and releasing effort from your back even more. *(long pause)*

# CANDLE MELT

*A soothing melt of tension.*

Get yourself comfortable, sitting supported or lying down.

Mentally scan your body, feel your body, noticing that tension creates a stiffness, a hardness in your body. *(pause)*

Visualize that stiffness, hard and inflexible, like candle wax.

Now bring awareness to the top of your head.

Visualize, and *feel* tension begin to soften and melt.

Whole scalp, face, jaw… melting.

Dripping down like candle wax.

Neck… shoulders… back… melting.

Arms and hands, melting, dripping down.

Hardness melting away.

Hips, legs, feet and toes, melting.

Until all that's left is a puddle.

All tension melted away. *(pause)*

Enjoy the sensation of tension melted, for a few breaths. *(long pause)*

Continue your day with more ease, reminding yourself to melt whenever you begin to feel tension.

# TENSION UNRAVELLING

*A quick practice to address tension in your body.*

Take a deep breath in…

And a long breath out.

Focus on an area of tension.

Inhale slowly into the area…

And exhale deeply, feeling as if the tension is unravelling, like a knitted sweater unravelling stitch by stitch.

Inhale slowly…

And deeply exhale tension, completely unravelling like a knitted sweater, by the end of the breath.

Inhale slowly.

And exhale deeply, tension completely unravelling.

Take a few breaths, enjoying the release.

Continue into your day, being mindful to stay relaxed.

# JAW MELT

*Relax a tense jaw.*

---

*Tip: Once you reach the final relaxed state in this one, you can also add the "Jaaaaw Soother" vibrations in the next meditation.*


Sit comfortably, with your back supported, slightly reclined. *(pause for settling)*

Mouth closed, take a deep breath in, sigh out.

Another breath in, long sigh out, mouth closed.

Breathe normally now.

Become aware of your lips.

Relax your jaw. *(pause)*

Notice your lips begin to move away from each other.

Nothing to do.

Relax your jaw. Allow your tongue to drop.

Just watching the lips.

Maybe lips begin to part.

Nothing to do. Simply noticing.

Relaxing the jaw.

Effortless.

Bring awareness to the jawbone between ear and chin.

Feel as if the whole area, both sides of your jaw are melting.

Softening. Sliding down. Dripping, as if they were warm wax.

The whole jaw, sliding down, away from the rest of the face.

Melting.

Maybe the mouth is agape now.

No need to do anything.

Just noticing.

Effortless.

Face and jaw are completely effortless.

If you like, continue to enjoy the effortlessness, for as long as you like.

Allow your eyelids to become heavy and if it feels good, let your eyes close. When you're ready, reopen your eyes. *(long pause)*

Gently close your mouth now, but allow your jaw to stay relaxed.

# JAAAAW SOOTHER

*Soothe a tense jaw with vibration.*

*Tip: You need to do this one out loud, so find a place where you won't disturb anyone. I like to do these in my car.*

Sit up comfortably, with or without back support. *(pause for settling)*

Relax your jaw and tongue.

Completely soften and relax your jaw and tongue.

Allow the mouth to fall open.

No effort at all.

Allow jaw and tongue to drop.

Begin to make a low, extended 'aw' sound.

Like the 'aw' in 'jaw'.

Aaaaaaaaaaw…

Loud enough to feel the vibration.

Effortless jaw and tongue.

No tension.

Keep going.

Aaaaaaaaaaw… extend it long.

No effort in the jaw or tongue.

Allow the sound to get lower.

Gravelly.

If the vibration and effortlessness feel soothing, continue.

When you're finished, hold for a few moments of silence, eyes closed.

Keep your jaw soft, for as long as you can remember to.

# HIGH-TONE HEADACHE HUM

*Soothe a headache with vibration.*

---

*Tip: You need to do this one out loud, so find a place where you won't disturb anyone. I like to do these in my car. You can also try this practice in a lower tone, to soothe your jaw.*

Sit up comfortably, with or without back support. *(pause for settling)*

Lips gently closed.

Tongue floating in the middle of your mouth.

Begin humming mmmmmm...

Keep the tongue free in the middle of the mouth.

Hum loud enough to feel the vibration in your head.

Keep humming.

Try a higher tone.

Mmmmmm...

Notice it changes where you feel the vibration in your head.

Try a lower tone.

Mmmmmm...

Notice where you feel it.

Keep humming.

Slowly raise the pitch.

Find the tone that feels best to your head tension.

Keep humming that tone.

Allow the vibration to break up the tension.

Soothing your head.

Resonating.

If the vibration feels soothing, continue.

When you're finished, hold for a few moments or minutes of silence, eyes closed.

# FULL BODY TENSION RELEASE

*Let go of tensions in your body, anytime.*

*Tip: This is also a great one to practice right before sleep.*

Get as comfortable and supported as possible so there's no need for your body to do anything. *(pause for settling)*

Begin by focusing attention on your feet.

All of your attention on your feet.

Allow your feet to soften, ease… relax. *(pause)*

And now focus all of your attention on your calves.

Allow your calves to soften, ease… relax. *(pause)*

Now your thighs.

Soften… ease… relax. *(pause)*

Hips.

Soften… ease… relax. *(pause)*

Your whole back.

Softening, relaxing. *(pause)*

Hands and arms.

Relax… *(pause)*

Shoulders, relax. *(pause)*

Neck relaxes. *(pause)*

Jaw and tongue. *(pause)*

Eyes… forehead… scalp. *(pause)*

Diving deeper now, inside the body.

Relax your stomach. *(pause)*

Heart. *(pause)*

Lungs. *(pause)*

Brain.

# DISCOMFORT DIFFUSING

*Diffuse discomfort in your body, anytime.*

*Tip: I use this practice to help manage my chronic pain.*

Mentally scan your body, looking for any one area that might feel tense, achy, dull or in any way is not feeling at its best. *(long pause)*

It's important to choose just one area at a time.

Bring undivided awareness to the one area.

Keep awareness there, but allow your awareness to diffuse.

Less focused, more diffused, like a cloud of awareness rather than a point. *(pause)*

Feel that as your awareness diffuses, the area of tension or dullness also disperses. *(pause)*

Tension, ache or dullness, breaking up. Dispersing. *(long pause)*

Taking relaxed breaths.

Effortless awareness on the body part.

Diffused.

Discomfort diffusing.

Continue breathing in this way for a few more breaths. *(long pause)*

Now if you like, repeat, bringing your awareness to another area that needs soothing.

Effortless awareness.

Diffused like a cloud.

As awareness diffuses, tension, ache or dullness diffuses. *(long pause)*

Repeat as many times as you like.

# FOR YOUR MIND

# OVERWHELM BALLOON BREATH

*Release the tense energy of overwhelm.*

Sitting comfortably, inhale slowly through the nose…

And exhale with pursed lips, loudly from the mouth.

Inhale softly through the nose.

Exhale loudly from the mouth.

Inhale gently, filling like a balloon.

Long exhale, deflating like a balloon, tension releasing.

Inhale gently.

Long exhale, softer now, through the mouth, deflating.

Slowing down…

Inhale gently.

Exhale, fully, comfortably, deflating tension.

Continue to breathe like this, deflating the tension of overwhelm.

When you feel better, breathe normally for a few breaths, before moving back into your day.

# SLOW YOUR ROLL

*Mind racing? Quickly slow yourself down, coming back to balance.*

Sitting comfortably, inhale deeply for a count of 1… 2… 3.

Exhale 1… 2… 3… 4.

Deep breath in through the nose, 1… 2… 3.

Exhale through the nose, 1… 2… 3… 4.

Slowing down…

Inhale 1…… 2…… 3.

Exhale 1…… 2…… 3…… 4.

Grounding…

Inhale 1…… 2…… 3.

Exhale 1…… 2…… 3…… 4.

Slowing down even more…

Inhale 1……… 2……… 3.

Exhale 1……… 2……… 3……… 4.

Continue for as long as you like, slower and slower with each breath.

# CATCH YOUR BREATH

*Anxiety making you short or shallow of breath? Try this.*

Sit or stand straight, chest lifted.

Take a breath in.

Now exhale for a slow count of 1… 2… 3… 4… 5.

Hold the breath out for a slow count of 1… 2… 3… 4… 5.

Release! Let air rush in.

Exhale slowly, everything out, 1… 2… 3… 4… 5… 6.

Hold the breath out, slowly count 1… 2… 3… 4… 5… 6.

Release! Let air in.

Exhale very slowly, emptying for 1… 2… 3… 4… 5… 6… 7.

Hold the breath out, slowly count 1… 2… 3… 4… 5… 6… 7.

Release!

Continue until you catch a good breath, increasing the number each time.

*Tip: It's important to really empty with each exhale, then completely release all holding to create a vacuum that automatically sucks air in, helping you feel that you've caught your breath.*

# WINDSWEPT

*Allow thoughts and tensions to be swept away.*

---

Get comfy, body and head supported. *(pause for settling)*

Allow your gaze to soften, eyelids to get heavy. *(pause)*

Jaw and shoulders relax. *(pause)*

Begin to feel as if a strong, steady wind is blowing toward you.

Blowing on your forehead.

The wind sweeps straight through – from your forehead, out the back of your head.

Steady, strong wind, sweeping through your head, taking with it any thoughts you were holding.

Clearing the clutter from the mind.

Expectations, worries – blown away.

Scattered by the wind. *(pause)*

Forehead windswept.

Mind windswept.

Mind cleared. *(long pause)*

Now feel the wind blowing through your whole body.

Powerful, strong, steady.

Wind blowing through your whole body from front to back.

Feel the wind take with it any tensions from your body.

Tensions blown away.

Scattered by the wind. *(long pause)*

You are left windswept.

Tensions cleared.

Mind clear.

Windswept. *(pause)*

Take a few relaxed breaths, feeling calm and clear.

# RIGHT HERE, RIGHT NOW

*Calm a worried or a racing mind.*

Get yourself into a comfortable position. Sitting or lying down, completely supported. *(pause until settled)*

Allow your eyelids to get heavy.

Right now, your body is supported.

You can release all tension, holding, and effort, into the support. *(pause)*

Right now, your body is breathing itself.

There's nothing you need to do. *(pause)*

Feel your body fully supported.

Let go of tension.

Notice your body breathing itself.

There's nothing you need to do right here, right now.

Settle into this moment of effortlessness. *(pause)*

Dive into the experience of non-doing, here and now.

Release all effort – here, and now. *(pause)*

There's nothing you need to do in these moments, right here, right now.

Take time to pause.

*Here* and *now. (long pause)*

# FREE YOUR MIND

*Release thoughts from a full mind to feel free and light.*

Inhaaaaale. Exhaaaaale.

Let your eyelids soften.

Allow your thoughts to begin to melt.

Thoughts losing structure… losing strength… losing importance.

As thoughts melt downward, feel your forehead soften, jaw soften.

Neck… back… arms… hands soften.

Legs and feet, soften.

Feel the last of the thoughts melt away, into the surface beneath you. *(long pause)*

Feeling light and emptied of thoughts.

Free from the *weight* of thought.

Thoughts are fully absorbed now, into the surface beneath you, spreading out, dissolving. *(pause)*

You are left light, free and peaceful. *(pause)*

Enjoy freedom from thought for a while, and when you're ready, continue your day with a freer, clearer mind.

# UNRAVELLING

*Get unstuck.*

---

Settle into a supported position, sitting or lying, where you can be comfortably still. *(pause for settling)*

Visualize yourself like a string-covered ornament.

Your soul, wrapped in one long string, in tidy rows.

Slowly tug at the tiny bit of string loose at the top.

The string begins to peel away.

Beautifully, gracefully, spiralling out.

Unravelling.

Unravelling *constructs of identity. (pause)*

Sigh out. Haaaaa

Unravelling further…

Unravelling *agendas. (pause)*

Sigh it out. *(pause)*

Unravelling more…

Unravelling *self-judgements,* and *expectations. (pause)*

Sigh it out. *(pause)*

Unravelling *fully* now.

And underneath, there you are.

Underneath it all, there you are.

Beautifully revealed.

Your pure self.

Your soul.

Free.

Limitless. *(pause)*

A sigh of relief.

A burst of excitement.

Free and limitless.

Dance, fly, express, play.

Feel this truth.

The freedom of your soul. *(long pause)*

Let that truth permeate all you do.

# ROOT GROUNDING

*Mind not quite grounded? Steady yourself.*

Sitting or lying supported, with your feet, seat or back resting on the floor.

Get comfortable. *(pause for settling)*

Begin to feel your body getting heavier.

Whole body, getting heavier.

Feel all energy moving downward, toward the earth beneath you.

Surrendered to gravity, energy and awareness moving downward.

*(Long pause)*

Feel as if tiny roots are growing, from whichever body parts are resting on the floor.

Feel the roots reaching toward the stable earth. *(long pause)*

Settling into the earth. *(pause)*

Notice the roots lengthening and growing thicker now.

More stable.

Deeper settled.

Settling into the earth.

Creating a strong and stable base for you to move freely above ground.

Steady support for your every movement.

Roots. Strong roots.

Feel the grounding… steadiness… support.

Strong.

Stable.

Settled. *(long pause)*

When you're ready, take a deep breath in, bringing awareness into your body.

Hold the sensation of being grounded, steady and supported.

Carry that feeling into the rest of your day.

# THE BIG EMPTY

*This is another simple technique for catching your breath if you're anxious or short of breath.*

Take a breath in.

And exhale empty…

Empty…

Empty…

Empty…

Empty…

Empty fully.

Hold the breath out, for as long as you can. *(long pause)*

Release – let air flow in.

And exhale empty…

Empty…

Empty…

Empty…

Empty…

Empty *everything out.*

Hold the breath out, for as long as you can. *(long pause)*

Release – let air flow in.

And exhale empty…

Empty…

Empty…

Empty…

Empty…

Empty completely.

Hold the breath out, *for as long as you can. (long pause)*

Release – let air flow in.

If you were able to catch a good, full breath, you're all set.

If not, and you feel comfortable, continue this exercise until you catch your breath and can regain a comfortable breathing pattern.

# GETTING PRESENT

*Draw your mind back from being stuck in the past or future.*

---

*Tip: You might like to follow up this mindfulness practice with the next one, "Finding Pleasant in the Present".*

Get comfortable, in any position. *(pause for settling)*

Allow your body to soften tension.

Shoulders relax.

Jaw, relax.

Eyelids get heavy.

Getting ready to bring awareness into the present, through the senses.

Start by listening for sounds.

Sounds nearby, sounds far away. *(pause)*

Listening.

What do you hear? *(long pause)*

Now begin to feel the surface beneath you.

Is it hard or soft? *(pause)*

Feel the texture of clothing on your skin.

Is it rough or smooth? *(pause)*

Feel the temperature of the air.

Is it hot, warm or cold? *(pause)*

Now, without moving your head, just your eyes, look around the room.

Notice the size of the room.

What objects can you see? *(pause)*

What colours? *(pause)*

Become aware of your tongue.

What do you taste? *(pause)*

And finally, is there any scent?

Scents near you, scents in the room?

Take deep breaths, using your sense of smell, identifying scents. *(long pause)*

Now noticing it all in this moment.

The sounds, sensations, sights, tastes and scents. *(pause)*

All of it here in this present moment.

Be aware of *yourself* here, in this present moment.

*(Long pause)*

# FINDING PLEASANT IN THE PRESENT

*If you're feeling dissatisfied or upset, look for the pleasant in the present.*

*Tip: This is a good mindfulness practice to do immediately after the previous one, "Getting Present".*

Looking for the pleasant in the present.

But without any pressure.

There's no way to get this wrong.

Simply exploring, free of judgements or expectation.

This is a journey, with no destination.

Things will be noticed, learned.

It's impossible to fail.

And the learning itself, is something pleasant to appreciate.

Beginning now, listen for something pleasant you hear.

It might be a sound, or lack of sound. *(pause)*

If you can't hear something pleasant, focus on any one thing you hear that gives you a neutral feeling.

Think about the source of that sound or lack of sound.

How is the sound being made? Who or what is making it? *(pause)*

Is there something pleasant you can find associated with the source of the sound? *(pause)*

If so, feel free to smile in appreciation if it feels good.

If not, that's fine too. Moving onto your sense of touch.

Noticing things you feel.

Textures, temperatures, support, sensations.

Is there something pleasant you feel here in the present? *(long pause)*

If so, if it feels good, allow a smile of appreciation.

If not, that's perfectly fine. Moving onto your sense of sight.

Noticing things you see.

Objects… colours… shapes… pattern… light… spaces.

Is there something pleasant you see here in the present? *(long pause)*

Smile if you like, appreciating.

If not, simply moving on, to your sense of taste.

Notice if you can taste anything.

Salty, sweet, bitter, pungent, sour.

**(cont'd...)**

Is there something pleasant you taste here in the present? *(long pause)*

Smiling if you like.

Moving on, to your sense of smell.

Noticing things you smell.

Scents in the room, the scent of your clothing, hair or body. Noticing any scent.

Is there something pleasant you smell here in the present? *(long pause)*

Smile if you like.

And taking a moment now, remembering the most pleasant thing you came across through your senses, or the pleasant feeling of simply being able to *experience* some or all of the senses. *(pause)*

Notice how your mind processed things – was it easy to find pleasant sensations… or challenging?

If it was challenging, this is a practice you can use to help strengthen your ability to look for the positive.

If it was easy, you can use this practice anytime you're feeling upset, to remind you of the pleasant things right here and now.

# COMING IN FOR LANDING

*Ground awareness in the present.*

---

Wherever you are, feel the support of the surface beneath you.

Let it hold you as you completely surrender to gravity.

Coming down from wherever your mind wandered off.

Awareness coming in for landing, here and now.

Observe the space around you.

Sights. *(pause)*

Sounds. *(pause)*

Sensations. *(pause)*

Being aware of where you are and what your senses are picking up with each passing moment.

You are *here*.

Landed in the present. *(pause)*

Inhale feeling present in this moment.

Exhale letting go of anything outside of this moment.

Inhale feeling present in this moment.

Exhale letting go of anything outside of right here, right now.

# TRUE FREEDOM (PURE AWARENESS)

*Rest body and mind. Return to the Source for freedom and peace.*

Make yourself as comfortable as possible in this moment, body and head fully supported. Getting ready to do nothing.

*(pause for settling)*

This time is just for you.

This practice is just for you.

There are no shoulds or shouldn'ts.

There's no way you can do this wrong.

This is about *you*.

This is for *you*.

Closely tune in to what your body or mind might need, to more fully relax in this moment.

Answer any request from your body or mind. All requests are equally welcome.

Do whatever you need, to feel supported, held, and free to let go of tensions. *(long pause)*

Your body and mind are astonishing, useful parts of your being, and yet, still, there is more to your self.

The deepest part of you is there through it all.

Aware of every experience.

Ever present.

Present in the experience of the physical body. Present when the body is resting.

Present in the experience of the mind. And even when the mind is resting, as in deep sleep.

There is a thread that remains. The essence of your being.

It is *awareness*. *(pause)*

Beyond body, energy, mind, you are *awareness*.

Pure awareness, without any trappings.

Unaffected by any state of body or mind.

Eternally peaceful and free. *(pause)*

Your essence, is peace.

You *are* peace.

*You* are the peace you've been looking for all along. *(pause)*

Rest now in the sublime beauty and peace that is you.

You in your deepest essence – pure awareness.

Eternally peaceful and free. *(pause)*

Rest in this state of true freedom.

Apart from body. Apart from mind.

Effortless.

Rest here for as long as you like, eyes open or closed.

# HELLO, FEAR.

---

*(I've found this practice helpful for managing panic disorder – the fear of fear. They're thoughts I've felt useful to read, repeat and internalize when I'm not panicked, so that when I'm on the verge of a panic attack, I can bring the simplest, most relevant words to mind – stealing the thunder from the panic attack and robbing it of its power over me.)*

Oh, hello, fear.

I see you.

Up to your old tricks again.

You're just a feeling. You can't hurt me.

You never do.

You're all bark and no bite.

I see you – but I'm not afraid of you.

I'm not going to try to escape.

I'm going to stay right here.

You can be here.

I know the drill.

You'll make sensations in my body.

Try to make me afraid.

Make me feel like I'm in danger.

I'm not in danger.

You'll make me feel like my body's going to collapse.

It never does.

Make me feel like it's the end of the world as I know it.

It's not.

It's all a show, all a lie.

Predictable and boring.

I never was in danger, and I'm not this time either.

Try to scare me all you want.

I'm not buying it.

I see you.

I know your tricks.

I'm not afraid.

I will sit with the sensations.

I will ride it out.

I will be absolutely fine.

# DAILY INSPIRATION FOR OTHERS

*Spark inspiration to give today.*

---

What will you share with the world today?

Your wisdom?

Humour?

Talent?

Helping hands?

Love?

Creativity?

What will you share, *today*?

Take a few deep breaths and see it.

Visualize it.

In vibrant, living colour.

You.

In your element.

Doing your best.

Sharing your gifts with the world.

# DAILY INSPIRATION FOR YOU

*Spark inspiration to **receive** today.*

Take a deep breath in, pulling in energy from all around you.

And slowly exhale.

Take a deep breath in, receiving energy.

And slowly exhale.

Take a moment to reflect. What will you do for yourself today?

Play? Pamper? Express? Nourish? Relax?

Maybe you'll clear things from your schedule or to-do list.

Or, have the perfect day of *no* agenda.

Maybe, you'd like to do *nothing at all. (pause)*

Choose just one thing to focus on. One thing for you. For today.

Take a few deep breaths and picture it:

You.

At the place.

Doing the thing.

For *you. (long pause)*

Enjoy your day.

# IN A PINCH

*A simple, memorable technique you can use any time to manage stress.*

Take a deeeeeep breath in.

And a looooooooong breath out.

Slowly inhaaaaaale…

And slowly exhaaale, softening your jaw.

Inhaaaaaale…

And exhaaale, soften your shoulders.

Inhaaaaaale…

And exhaaale, soften your whole upper body.

Inhaaaaaale…

And exhaaale, soften your whole lower body.

Entire body is relaxed.

Hold that feeling, staying relaxed.

*(Repeat if needed.)*

# FOR ENERGY

# ENERGY DRINK

*Perfect for a tired body after hard work.*

---

Resting comfortably, relaxed and fully supported.

Make sure you're set up in such a way that your body doesn't need to make any effort.

The whole body supported; welcome to rest comfortably.

Get as comfortable as possible. *(pause for settling)*

Now that you're comfy, become aware of your nostrils.

Take a few deep breaths in, focusing on the inhalation. *(long pause)*

Feel that as you breathe in, you're sucking in energy.

Through the nostrils.

Like two straws, drinking in energy. *(pause)*

Now purse your lips as if they're around a straw, and exhale through your mouth.

Inhaling gently, slowly, through the nostrils.

Exhaling gently, slowly, through pursed lips.

Inhaling, drinking in energy.

Exhaling any fatigue. Let it flow out.

Inhale, through the nose, filling up with energy.

Exhale, out the mouth, fatigue flowing out.

Take your time, continuing to breathe this way, energy in, fatigue out.

Allow the breath to become softer and softer.

Once you're feeling a little more energized, less fatigued, take normal, relaxed breaths, through the nose only, or however you normally breathe.

Fatigue released.

Energy taken in.

Close your eyes if you like and enjoy the shift in energy, feeling more balanced.

# WHOLE BODY BREATHING

*Become calm and energized, all at once.*

---

Getting settled in any comfortable position.

Become aware of the whole front side of your body.

The whole front of your body, from your toes to the top of your head. *(pause)*

Now become aware of the back side of your body.

The whole back side of the body from head to toes. *(pause)*

Now become aware of the whole right side of your body.

The whole right side of the body. *(pause)*

Shift awareness to the left side of your body.

Be aware of the whole left side of the body. *(pause)*

Awareness of the whole body together.

The whole body together.

The whole body together.

Awareness diffused over the whole body. *(long pause)*

Feel as if the whole body is breathing.

Energy coming in, energy going out.

A field of energy.

Energy outside and inside your body, in a continual, effortless exchange.

Whole body, breathing.

Whole body, alive with energy. *(long pause)*

Continue with the rest of your day, holding this calm, yet energized state, for as long as you can.

Return to this practice anytime you need.

*Tip: If you'd like to increase awareness of your energy, continue with the next meditation, "You're Electric".*

# YOU'RE ELECTRIC

*Tune in, to your electric nature.*

Resting comfortably… relaxed.

Whole body, sinking into the support beneath you.

Nothing for you to do.

Allow your body to ease.

Be aware of your whole body all at once.

Aware of your whole body as a field of energy.

Feel as if your whole body is breathing.

Entire body, effortlessly breathing.

Nothing to do.

Simply observing.

The whole body breathing, effortlessly.

Breathing through every pore.

Energy flowing effortlessly in, permeating the body.

Alive with energy.

Effortless flow of energy.

In and out.

You are electric.

Visualize or feel this in any way you like.

Light, sparks, currents or anything else that pops into mind.

Your whole body, alive with energy.

Electric.

Buzzing.

There's nothing you need to do.

Your whole body is alive with energy, at every moment of every day.

Be aware of that reality.

Energy is dancing around, buzzing around, inside your body, at every moment.

At every moment.

It's a fact.

You might not feel that energy at every moment.

You might feel you lack energy.

Tune in.

Energy *is* there.

At *every* moment.

If it feels helpful, bring awareness to this fact of your electric nature, anytime you need.

You can increase the sensation of feeling electric by getting fresh air, fresh fruit, or a glass of water.

# FRESH AIR

*Take your fatigue outside.*

This one is very simple.

One of the best ways to instantly lift your energy is to get some fresh air.

So, crack a window open, a door, or better yet, get outside to sit or take a walk.

If you like, be mindful of the fresh air you're taking in.

Energy coming in with each inhale.

Or simply do nothing and allow your body to breathe, doing all the work for you.

Fresh air is an effortless way to re-energize.

Even if it's fresh *city* air!

# LIGHTENING UP

*Shift from heavy energy – fatigue, overwhelm, sadness – to lighter energy.*

Awakening to the sensation of lightness in the body.

Feel that every part of the body is filling up with lightness, like a helium balloon.

Body becoming lighter and lighter.

The right leg becoming light, lifting up.

Left leg, filling up with lightness and floating right up.

The right arm becoming lighter and lighter, picking up.

The left arm becoming light, floating up.

The hips and torso becoming light, filling up like a helium balloon, and floating right up.

And finally, the head, filling with the sensation of lightness, floating right up.

Entire body, floating. Light as air.

Experience lightness throughout the entire body. Absolute lightness. *(long pause)*

Now gently release the feeling of floating. Coming down, grounded once again, but holding the sensation of lightness.

# RELAX TO RE-ENERGIZE

*Stop tension from draining your energy.*

*Tip: This can be done anywhere, anytime, doing any activity. I like to practice this while walking, holding yoga poses or doing household chores. For your first time, try walking while reading this meditation.*

We often hold tension without realizing it.

Bring awareness into your body.

Scan for any areas of tension, holding, tightness, effort.

Could you make any of those areas soften, loosen, let go or use less effort?

Focus on one body part at a time, releasing tension, using a little less effort.

If you're moving, this might mean you slow down your actions. Are there any body parts that are tense that don't need to be?

Sometimes it's the jaw, shoulders, hands.

Any unnecessary, unhelpful tension – soften, release, melt, let go. *(long pause)*

Be aware that tension is stealing your energy.

Tension is stealing your energy.

To reduce this energy loss, release extra effort. Release tension.

Allow your body to fall into a state of more ease.

Loose, flexible, flowing.

Energy flowing, effortlessly.

Moving toward a state of ease.

The more effortless you become, the more easily energy flows, the easier the action feels.

The more effortless you become, the less energy is expended.

The more energy you conserve for the rest of your day.

Allow your body to settle into ease.

Energy flowing freely.

Action becomes fluid.

Even the mind becomes calmer. *(pause)*

Body and mind at ease, while active in the world.

# NOTHING TIME

*Recharge with some time doing absolutely nothing.*

Getting comfy, ready for the practice of doing nothing.

Be sure your body and head are supported, comfortable, and can fully let go of tension. *(pause for settling)*

You spend so much time doing, thinking.

For now, you can simply *be*.

Nothing you need to do.

Nothing asked of you.

No agenda.

No goal.

No way to do this wrong.

Just peace.

Just *being*. *(pause)*

Give yourself permission to let go of all effort in your body.

Let go of all effort, all tension. *(pause)*

Give yourself permission to rest.

Simply *rest*. *(pause)*

Nothing you need to do.

No way to get this wrong.

Just you.

Just peace.

Just *being*.

Even the mind can rest now.

Close your eyes and take as much "nothing time" as you like.

# BREATHING WITH TREES

*Re-connect with our planet's natural, harmonious energy exchange.*

---

Imagine you are sitting among trees.

In a forest, in a park – anywhere you like, where there are trees. *(long pause)*

Among the trees, become aware of your breath.

You natural breath, just as it is.

Notice that with each effortless inhale, you draw in fresh air and energy. *(pause)*

Every effortless inhale, drawing in fresh air and energy. *(pause)*

As you exhale, you release a gift for the trees – carbon dioxide.

The trees happily breathe in this carbon dioxide. *(pause)*

And in exchange, the trees breathe out oxygen, a gift for *you*. *(pause)*

Noticing this perfect, beautiful exchange.

Effortlessly, you breathe in the gift from the trees – energizing oxygen.

And effortlessly as you exhale, you give energy to the trees.

Breathing in energy.

Breathing out energy.

Effortless. *(pause)*

Breathing in, receiving.

Breathing out, giving.

Effortless. *(pause)*

Continue to be aware of this perfect, effortless, harmonious exchange between you and the trees, for the next few moments or minutes.

# DOWN & OUT GROUNDING

*Worried or stomach in knots? Move nervous energy down and out.*

---

Sit in a squat or a tucked position with knees toward you.

Take a slow, deep breath in…

And a long, slow breath out.

Slow, deep breath in…

And as you exhale, feel as if nervousness, uncertainty, upset moves down and out.

Deep breath in…

And exhale nervousness, uncertainty, upset down and out.

Deep breath in…

And exhale any discomfort, down and out.

Continue to breathe in this way as many times as you'd like or until you feel more grounded and calmer.

# BREATHING IN MORNING ENERGY

*A simple practice to energize your morning.*

In any comfortable position, become aware of the light in the room.

The morning light.

Charged with energy and potential. *(pause)*

Take a moment to breathe in the morning light with your whole body. *(pause)*

Soaking in its energy and potential. *(pause)*

Soaking in the beauty of the morning light with your whole being. *(pause)*

Observing this simple breath for the next minute.

Breathing in the beauty, energy and potential of the morning light, with your whole body.

If you like, close your eyes.

# BREATHING IN EVENING ENERGY

*A simple practice to wind down for the night.*

---

In any comfortable position, bring awareness to your ribcage.

Notice the ribcage expanding and contracting as your body breathes.

No need to make any changes to the breath.

Simply noticing the natural expansion and contraction of the ribcage as your body breathes. *(long pause)*

Now bring awareness to the air moving in and out of the body.

Follow the air as it moves in through the nostrils, down to the lungs, and follow the air as it moves up and out through the nostrils.

Follow the movement of the air.

Watching the air. *(long pause)*

Continue watching the air.

The subtle quality of the air, as it moves in and out of the body.

Awareness of the *subtle quality* of the air. *(pause)*

Now allowing awareness to dissolve, into the *space* in which the air is moving.

Awareness dissolving, into the *space* in which the air is moving.

The space inside the body. *(pause)*

The space around the body. *(pause)*

Allow awareness to dissolve into the subtlest quality, of space. *(pause)*

Awareness dissolving into space.

The quality of space. Still. Effortless. All-pervading, space.

If it feels peaceful, allow awareness to rest now in this quality of still, effortless space for the next minute.

# FOR EMOTIONS AND FEELINGS

# SMILE LIFTER

*Lift your spirits. Whether you find this meditation inspiring or silly, either way you'll end up smiling.*

Inhale slowly, rising the corners of your lips, ever so slightly.

Deep, slow exhale as you hold that subtle smile.

Inhale deeply, corners of your lips rise a little bit more.

Long exhale, holding that gentle smile.

Inhale, corners of your lips rising even further.

Slow exhale, softly holding that smile.

Deep inhale, smiling.

Exhale, feel your smile radiating warmth and light through your whole body.

Inhale, softly smiling.

Exhale radiating warmth and light through your whole body

Inhale, smiling.

Exhale radiating warmth and light all around you.

Close your eyes and pause for a few moments of silence.

# SMOKE

*Clear the funk of unpleasant feelings.*

Take a deep, long breath in.

Now slowly exhale, for even longer than you inhaled.

Inhale slowly, deeply.

And exhale any unpleasant feelings, like dark smoke leaving you, dispersing, disappearing.

Hold the breath out, seeing the air around you cleared.

Now take a deep breath in, of the clear air.

Exhale unpleasant feelings, like dark smoke, dispersing, disappearing, away from you.

Hold the breath out, see the air cleared. *(pause)*

Take a deep, cleansing breath in.

Exhale any remaining unpleasantness as smoke.

Hold, seeing clear air around you. *(pause)*

Cleansing breath in.

Continue for as long as you like, exhaling unpleasantness like smoke, seeing it cleared, taking cleansing breaths in.

You can use this technique to release unpleasant feelings, anytime you need.

# SIGH IT OUT

*Unruffle yourself – let it out in a sigh.*

---

*Tip: Sighing can be really helpful. I'm a big sigher. I do it often, and people will say, "Are you ok?" And I respond, "Yes, thanks, I'm great", because I've just released a huge clump of built-up tension.*

Sometimes things don't go our way.

If it's happened now, take a deep breath in and…

Sigh it out. *(pause)*

Deep breath in, and try a big, ugly, gruff sigh…

Deep breath in, and try a loud, desperate, pained sigh…

Deep breath in, and try a quiet, calming, soft sigh…

Try whatever flavor of sigh the moment calls for.

Sigh it out.

Take it up and out.

Release it.

# REFRESHING STREAM

*Wash away unpleasant feelings and move forward,*
*refreshed.*

---

Visualizing a stream of water, pouring down the back of your head, from the crown, down to the shoulders, down the back, and away from you.

The perfect temperature – hot, warm or cool – whatever feels soothing in this moment.

Flowing in a constant steady stream. *(pause)*

From the crown of your head, past the shoulders, down the back, down and away from you.

Washing away all unpleasant feelings, tensions, worries.

All unpleasant feelings, tensions, worries, washed away. *(pause)*

All of it – washed away.

Stream of water, pouring down, from the crown of the head, past the shoulders, down the back, down and away from you.

Constant, steady stream.

Refreshing you.

Heart, body and mind.

Refreshed.

Take a moment to enjoy the feeling of this steady stream refreshing you. *(long pause)*

You can start fresh from this moment on.

Fresh feeling.

Fresh outlook.

Fresh sensation from head to toe.

Ready to start fresh from this moment on.

Continue into your day, refreshed.

# WEIGHT OF THE WORLD, DIFFUSING

*Lighten your burden as you expand your sense of Self.*

Getting very comfortable.

Body completely supported, sitting reclined or lying down.

Allow your eyes to get heavy.

Face dropping any tension.

Shoulders dropping.

Dropping into the support beneath you.

Diffuse awareness over the whole body.

Aware of the whole body all at once. *(pause)*

Feel as if the whole body is breathing.

Energy coming in, energy going out. *(pause)*

A field of energy.

Energy outside and inside your body, in a continual, effortless exchange.

Divinely enmeshed, entwined, energy dancing within and without.

Expand your sense of Self, beyond the borders of your body.

Expanding field of energy. *(pause)*

The line between "inside" of you and "outside" of you, blurring.

The line between "you" and "the world" blurring, diffusing. *(pause)*

A field of energy.

Within and without.

In a constant, cosmic dance.

As awareness expands beyond the body into the field of energy, notice that any discomfort associated with the body diffuses and dissolves.

Awareness of the body *and its discomfort* – left behind.

No longer held. *(pause)*

As awareness expands, your sense of Self expands.

Worries associated with this body, this mind, diffuse and dissolve.

Awareness expands, worry left behind.

No longer held. *(pause)*

All concerns diffusing, dissolving, as awareness merges into the field of energy.

Heaviness turning to lightness.

**(cont'd...)**

Burden turning to freedom.

As you expand your awareness of Self.

If it feels good, dive into this expanded awareness.

Energetic awareness.

Allowing your Self to take up as much space as you like.

Take your time.

Pause here for a few moments or minutes. *(long pause for experiencing)*

Take a couple of deep breaths, bringing awareness back into your body.

If it feels good, hold some sense of your expanded Self and your ability to revisit that awareness anytime you like.

# IN MY BUBBLE

*Create a beautiful boundary.*

---

Bring awareness to the centre of your body. *(pause)*

Visualize a teeny, clear bubble there. Small as one tiny soap bubble.

With each inhale, you can expand that bubble.

Picture your tiny, clear bubble.

Inhale, fill it to the size of a bubble gum bubble.

Exhale, see it clear, shiny and gum-bubble-sized.

Deep inhale, fill it to the size of a balloon.

Long exhale, see it clear, shiny and wobbling. Balloon-sized.

Deep inhale now, bubble rapidly expands until your whole body is encircled.

Long exhale, beautiful, bouncy bubble surrounding you.

Deep inhale, peaceful in your bubble, flexible and strong.

Long exhale, watch negative energy bouncing off.

Allow your breath to become easy now, as you rest in your flexible, strong, resilient bubble.

Stay in your bubble for as long as you like, or pop it anytime you like.

It's your bubble. Use it as you like. Your beautiful, bouncy bubble. *(pause for silence)*

# MOTHER EARTH'S EMBRACE

*When you just need a hug. You can return to this practice anytime you need, to feel comforted and supported.*

---

*Tip: If you have the opportunity, this one is especially powerful outside, lying on the earth.*

Find a spot on the floor or ground, where you can comfortably lie or sit down.

If it's comfortable, lie on your abdomen, making a pillow with your hands, resting your head to the side. If it's not comfortable, you can lie on your back or side, or sit supported.

Once you're comfortable, take a deep breath in, and sigh it out.

Allow your body to let go of any effort against gravity.

Peacefully, let go to gravity.

Allow yourself to be held by Mother Earth.

Unconditionally.

Release all body tension to Mother Earth.

Let her hold it for you. *(long pause)*

Release all worries to Mother Earth.

She will hold them for you. *(long pause)*

Release any heavy emotion or heaviness in your heart.

Mother Earth will hold it. *(long pause)*

Mother Earth is holding you.

Supporting you.

Unconditionally.

Always.

Always here for a hug, whenever you need it.

No judgement.

No expectations.

No strings attached.

Mother Earth is here for you, anytime you need.

To hold your burdens.

To give you steady support.

To listen.

If you'd like to speak heart to heart with Mother Earth, or ask for guidance, take a moment to do that now. If not, simply enjoy Mother Earth's embrace for as long as you need.

When you're done, give thanks for these comforting moments in Mother Earth's embrace. *(pause for silence.)*

# YOU'RE DOING IT!

*Inspiration for your future self and a smile for your current self.*

---

What would you really like to do at some future time?

Think on it for a moment.

Maybe a goal, an experience, an adventure.

Simple or big.

Anything you'd like to do some time in the future, whether it's a week away, a year away or later today.

Something that makes you smile just thinking about it. *(pause)*

Visualize yourself doing it.

Where are you?

What does the place look like? *(pause)*

What do *you* look like? *(pause)*

What are you doing?

How are you feeling? *(pause)*

Are there others there?

What does it sound like? *(pause)*

Are there any scents or tastes?

Allow it to play out in your mind.

Feel all the joy of it. *(pause)*

There you are – you're doing it! *(long pause)*

Know that each moment you spend visualizing it brings a smile to your face right now.

It also plants a seed in your awareness that can help make it a future reality.

Enjoy daydreaming about it for as long as you like.

# BE A FRIEND

*Struggling? Be a friend to yourself.*

Looking with the eyes of a compassionate observer, visualize yourself as you are right now. *(pause)*

See where you are. *(pause)*

What you're wearing. *(pause)*

Your posture. *(pause)*

Your facial expression. *(pause)*

See yourself, right now, as you are, from an outside perspective.

From a compassionate perspective.

As a compassionate outsider, how do you feel about this person? *(pause)*

What kind words do you have for this person? *(long pause)*

Do you have any words of wisdom or suggestions for this person? *(long pause)*

Let this person know you see them… and love them. *(long pause)*

Feel the kind words and love given to you and hold it close.

Know that you can use this meditation to offer yourself compassion and support, anytime you need.

# COURAGEOUS CONFIDENCE

*You are supported at every moment. Be courageous.*

Get comfy, in any position. Body and head supported, if possible. *(pause for settling)*

Bring awareness to your breath.

Your natural breath, nothing for you to do.

Feel your body naturally expand and contract, without you doing anything. *(pause)*

Body is taking care of your breath for you, all by itself.

There's nothing you need to do.

For a moment, simply be aware of this miracle of your body undertaking all the complex processes of breathing, with grace and without expectation. *(long pause)*

You are supported by your body.

Cared for by your body.

Every moment of your life.

Your body is doing its best for you.

You are supported by this breath at every moment in your life.

**(cont'd...)**

Supported by the *intelligence* behind the breath at every moment in your life.

Supported by the *energy fuelling the intelligence,* at every moment in your life.

At every moment of your life.

Supported effortlessly, by miraculous intelligence and energy. The wind beneath your wings.

Soar high. Be free. Be bold.

Soar high. Be free. Be bold.

You are supported at every moment by a higher intelligence. Supported effortlessly with energy.

Spread your wings and fly. All the conditions are there. If you falter, the conditions will still be there, and you can try again. *(pause)*

You are always supported by a higher intelligence and energy. There is a current already there to lift you up. Allow the current to lift you, high into the sky, soaring. *(pause)*

This is the nature of your being. You are always supported by a higher intelligence and energy, at every moment.

The very same intelligence and energy supporting every person, animal, blade of grass.

Experience this connection to higher intelligence, energy, constant support.

Experience this connection in any way you like. Visualizing or feeling… soaring, supported, miraculous potential.

Experience this connection to higher intelligence, energy, constant support in any way you like.

Let it fuel the sensation of effortless confidence and courage. *(pause)*

Experiencing this in any way you like, for the next few moments or minutes. *(long pause for visualizing)*

# COLOUR SOOTHING

*Soothe uncomfortable feelings with colourful light.*

Allow your body to soften and relax.

Allow your eyelids to get heavier, gaze softer.

Picture yourself in a ray of light.

Shining over your whole body.

A ray of light, in a beautiful, soothing colour. *(long pause)*

Your whole body, bathing in colourful, soothing light.

Breathe in that soothing colour.

Take it in, with every pore of your body.

Every part of your being.

Soaking in soothing light.

Filling your body, your whole self, with colourful light.

Lightening the sensation of your body.

Lightening your mood.

Illuminating your mind.

Lightening your spirit.

Your whole self, *light*.

Soothed.

Glowing.

Your entire being, glowing, radiant, with colourful, soothing light. *(pause)*

Allow yourself to become immersed in the experience.

Close your eyes and enjoy for a few extra moments, or minutes. *(long pause for experiencing)*

And now continue your day with this new sensation of lightness and feeling soothed.

# INNER EXCURSION

*A mental, mini vacation.*

---

Choosing a position where your heart feels open. Open for this getaway to make your heart sing. *(pause for settling)*

Taking a pause from your day.

Headed for a well-deserved getaway.

Allow your body to get comfortable.

You can relax now, on your mini vacation.

Allow your eyelids to get heavy, gaze softening.

Attention is drawing inward.

Inhale, taking in the sweetness of this moment.

Exhale letting go into the comfort.

Inhale feeling grateful for this getaway.

Exhale releasing into the comfort, even more. *(pause)*

Allow your mind to wander into thoughts of your vacation destination.

Where will you go to feel at ease… to relax and recharge?

It could be anywhere. A beach, a cottage, a room in a home, a place of beauty or interest.

Choose any place you like, remembered or imagined. *(long pause)*

Picture yourself there, as vividly as you can. What do you see? *(long pause)*

What are the colours and quality of light? *(pause)*

What does it sound like? *(long pause)*

What does it smell like? *(long pause)*

What does it feel like? *(long pause)*

Picture it in great detail. See and *feel* yourself experiencing it. *(long pause)*

And now, in this beautiful place, take a minute to enjoy yourself here. Relax and recharge, in any way you like.

Pause here for a few moments or minutes. *(long pause for visualizing)*

And now, taking with you any positive feelings from your getaway, say goodbye for now.

Knowing your vacation spot is always here for you.

You can return whenever you like.

Coming back now, into the room.

Bringing positive feelings with you.

Back, into the here and now.

Relaxed, refreshed and ready for the rest of your day.

# YOU'RE ALLOWED

*Give yourself permission and find your freedom – just as you are.*

See yourself for a moment, as if you were an outside observer.

If it feels good, speak kindly to yourself, saying mentally:

*You're allowed. (pause)*

You're allowed to feel bad.

You're allowed to feel good.

You're allowed to do.

You're allowed to not do.

You're allowed to be sure.

You're allowed to be unsure.

You're allowed to be tired.

You're allowed to rest.

You're allowed to be quiet.

You're allowed to be loud.

You are allowed.

To be as you are.

Right now.

Without judgement.

Without expectation.

Without guilt or denial.

You are allowed.

To be just as you are.

In this moment.

In every moment.

*(Pause for silence.)*

# FREE GIFT!

---

## 3 Audio Meditations

Let me lull you into sweet relaxation and peace with three of my most popular meditations, sent to you as mp3s:

- Smile Lifter
- Candle Melt
- Slow Your Roll

**Get them now, at:**

**tamaraskyhawk.com/free.**

# REVIEWS APPRECIATED!

**Enjoy the book?**

Sharing a review on Amazon is incredibly helpful in spreading the goodness. Help more people learn about the book and benefit.

**Leave your review on Amazon now!**

With much gratitude,

**Tamara**

# OTHER BOOKS

**by Tamara Skyhawk**

### Yoga Nidra Scripts

22 Meditations for Effortless Relaxation,
Rejuvenation and Reconnection

### Yoga Nidra Scripts 2

22 More Meditations for Effortless Relaxation,
Rejuvenation and Reconnection

### Affirmations for Queens

99 Pep Talks for Self-Confidence,
Magnificence and Phenomenal Gloriosity

### Are You a Tomato?

A Silly, Interactive Book to Help Kids Build
Confidence in Their Self-Identity and Resilience to Bullying

### Mother Nature's Whisper

A Kids' Book to Inspire a Love of Nature and Outdoor Play

### All available on Amazon.

Learn more about these and upcoming books at
tamaraskyhawk.com.

Made in United States
North Haven, CT
15 October 2023

42769185R10069